S0-BUB-093

Over the Water:
Fujiko Nakaya

This catalog was published to accompany the Exploratorium's inaugural project *Over the Water: Fujiko Nakaya*, on view at Pier 15, San Francisco, from April 17 to October 6, 2013.

Editors:
Leigh Markopoulos
Marina McDougall

Publication Manager:
Leigh Markopoulos

Design:
John Borruso

Printer:
Solstice Press, Oakland

This publication is available for free download: http://www.exploratorium.edu/arts/over-the-water

© 2013, the authors, Fujiko Nakaya, Exploratorium, Pier 15, San Francisco, CA 94111, and copyright holders as listed. No part of this publication may be reproduced in any manner without permission.

All photographs of *Fog Bridge #72494*, 2013 © Exploratorium Cover, back cover, inside cover, and pages 22–25 Photos: Gayle Laird

The arts at the Exploratorium are generously funded in part by grants from the National Endowment for the Arts and the San Francisco Hotel Tax Fund.

ART WORKS.
arts.gov

grants | for the
Arts
San Francisco Hotel Tax Fund

ISBN: 978-0-943451-70-1

expl◯ratorium

Exploratorium
Pier 15
San Francisco, CA 94111
www.exploratorium.edu

CONTENTS

OVER THE WATER
Tom Rockwell

The Exploratorium at Piers 15 and 17 sits on the edge of the San Francisco Bay, perched at the juncture where the water meets the bustling Embarcadero. Our new site lives at a boundary between a designed, urban space filled with people and a much more natural, if occasionally alien, world of changing tides, churning sediments, and microscopic life. We are delighted to celebrate our relocation with the launch of *Over the Water*, an innovative, site-specific public art program. First with our opening, and then annually, we will invite a contemporary artist or designer to interpret the ways in which our site's multiple environments, at once physical, biological, and social, interact. It is fitting then that we inaugurate this program with *Fog Bridge* by Fujiko Nakaya, an artist whose works situate people, places, and fog in unexpected juxtapositions.

At its core the Exploratorium has always privileged the encounter between human experience and natural phenomena. A good exhibit about physics can awaken the senses and provoke an embodied curiosity; our best exhibits create an opportunity for dialogue between an inquiring mind and the natural world. *Fog Bridge* continues this tradition but on a larger scale, bringing into relief the interaction of air, water, light, and perception in the environment to create a multi-layered experience. On a purely physical level this piece is simply water floating in air, interacting with light. But add a human witness and it becomes a dynamic art piece, one that sculpts fog, air, and light for visual and sensorial pleasure. Fluid dynamics, states of matter, optics, and meteorology, as well as human perception and intellect, are all connected in this staged phenomenon.

But there is more. This mist doesn't come rolling in from the ocean, over the hills, like the fog we know so well in San Francisco. Instead, it bursts from nozzles mounted on a bridge, itself a built structure and an unlikely source of fog. So, yes, it is about fog as a natural and perceptual phenomenon. But it is also about the play of architecture, engineering, and nature disrupting our expectations as to how

Fujiko Nakaya
Fog Bridge
#72494, 2013.
Exploratorium,
San Francisco,
California.
Photo: Amy Snyder
© Exploratorium

the built and natural environments interact. The fog momentarily de-solidifies the hard materials of the bridge, obscuring its structure and passengers. It changes not only our physical sensations, but also our social and emotional expectations, as structure and people disappear from view and our sense of place is disrupted by an improbable curtain.

It is this interplay of physics, perception, place, and social inter-action that makes *Fog Bridge* such a felicitous opening installation for our new site. With our relocation to the Embarcadero and with the launch of *Over the Water*, we hope to extend beyond the walls of our institution to support civic and artistic spaces that afford public engagement. Whereas in the past ancient temples or baroque fountains anchored public gathering spaces, today museums and art installations serve as dynamic civic catalysts. *Fog Bridge*, together with many of our other outdoor exhibits, is located in the publicly accessible area that winds around and through the new Exploratorium campus. Here, we offer a public space to San Francisco, a plaza to surprise and engage passers-by, sparking new insights and conversa-tions. Every year, we hope those who live in or visit the Bay Area will come to anticipate a new artistic transformation of this unique site between the city and the water.

ACKNOWLEDGEMENTS
Marina McDougall

> *My work always grows because of the exposure to engineers;*
> *their collaboration has been an enormous artistic contribution.*
>
> Robert Rauschenberg

This project would not have been possible without the generosity and hard work of a number of collaborators—some of their names appear on page forty-eight—and they have our sincere gratitude. In addition, we'd like to take this opportunity to highlight the contributions of a few key individuals who were instrumental in realizing this first iteration of the *Over the Water* program.

Fog Bridge would not exist without the hard work and thoughtful planning of a good number of engineers. We would like to thank Thomas Mee and D'Arcy Sloane of Mee Industries, the long time collaborators of Fujiko Nakaya, for generously partnering with us on this project. We are also grateful to Dave Sola at Mee who has been invaluable as an adviser throughout the development of the project.

The Exploratorium is deeply enriched by the expertise of many engineers on our staff. We would particularly like to thank Dave Johnson, the project manager for his contribution towards this ambitious undertaking. The project involved creating water and electrical infrastructure at Pier 17 during the challenge of the Exploratorium's move to its new campus. Dave has navigated this complex process and overseen every last technical detail with skill and good humor and we could not have pulled it all off without him. We also extend our special thanks to Vicente Jimenez for his excellent work in plumbing Pier 17.

We would like to thank Leigh Markopoulos, an engineer of another sort, for her thoughtful insight as a contributor to, and the managing editor of, this catalog. Leigh has been a wonderful collaborator on the project and her research has deepened our understanding of Nakaya's profound contributions as an artist. We would also like to thank John Borruso for his handsome design of this publication.

6

Exploratorium Outdoor Studio staff installing *Fog Bridge* at high tide. Photo: Marina McDougall, 2013

Henry Urbach has been a great admirer of Fujiko Nakaya for many years and his recommendation of her work for our inaugural *Over the Water* commission at our new waterfront site could not have been better.

Exploratorium Trustee Bill Fisher has encouraged us to animate our presence at Pier 15 with a robust arts program. We are grateful for his visionary leadership, and for the enthusiasm and insights that he continues to bring to our work at the Exploratorium. We look forward to his collaboration on future projects.

Most of all we would like to extend our deep gratitude to Fujiko Nakaya for *Fog Bridge*, a work that sets an exciting precedent for the future of our *Over the Water* program.

It has been an extraordinary privilege to work with Nakaya, a true pioneer whose practice grows out of such a rich history and remains so generative. Her generosity as a collaborator continues to be deeply inspirational.

Andy Black and Sam Green, *Fog City*, 2013. Production photo: Andy Black

LEARNING TO LOVE THE FOG
Marina McDougall

San Francisco environmental journalist Harold Gilliam has written compellingly about the complex geological and climatic conditions that combine to produce Bay Area fog:

> Shaped by the slant of the California coastline and the oceanic currents of wind and water, by the presence of a strait and estuary penetrating the coastal mountain ranges, by the hill and valley contours of San Francisco and the region around the bay, the advance of the summer fog inland from the Pacific is one of the planet's most awesome natural spectacles.[1]

This spectacle is perhaps best appreciated from a distance. The sight of fog cascading over Twin Peaks when observed from the safe remove of Potrero Hill is truly extraordinary. A vast ocean of fog drifting south over the Pacific towards the mouth of the Golden Gate when seen from the heights of Mount Tamalpais can stir a sense of wonder, even in the middle of July. But the experience of driving back to the city from that privileged vantage point and traversing the all-pervasive grey wall of low-lying cloud, known to specialists as *stratus nebulosus* fog, is another matter.

Though we San Francisco natives are well accustomed to these annual cycles of fog, we still cannot fully shake the expectation of a hot summer season. As a result, rather than celebrating this spectacular natural feature, the city on the whole seems to have an ambivalent relationship to fog. Tourist literature underplays the drama of the local weather and tourists are regularly caught unexpectedly by the fog, making polar fleece outerwear one of San Francisco's most popular souvenirs.

Tokyo-based artist Fujiko Nakaya has been creating fog environments around the world for over forty years, yet she confesses that she was somewhat hesitant to develop a project for San Francisco given the local competition. However, this city has numerous microclimates and while fog makes regular appearances near the ocean, it visits

Dr. Ukichiro Nakaya working in a cold chamber at the Low Temperature Laboratory, Hokkaido University, 1936. Image courtesy of Fujiko Nakaya

the downtown waterfront, the new home of the Exploratorium, less frequently. For six months over the spring and summer of 2013, Nakaya is artificially creating a microcosmic experience of fog in a warm pocket on the Embarcadero. By doing so, she hopes to provoke an appreciation of San Francisco fog in all its magnificent and varied forms.

A fascination with the element of water, whether solid, liquid, or gas, runs in Nakaya's family. Her father, snow physicist and science essayist Ukichiro Nakaya, was a founder of, and pioneer in, the field of glaciology.[2] The Nakaya Ukichiro Museum of Snow and Ice in Kaga City, Japan, commemorates his work. He is celebrated for growing the first artificial snow crystal in 1936 and for developing the Nakaya Diagram, a general classification system for snow crystals based on the observation and micro-photography of over 3,000 specimens over the course of three winters.[3]

Nakaya's artistic practice entails similarly rigorous research at the intersection of natural phenomena and engineering. Her work centers on observation, an activity important to both artists and scientists, and her subject is fog's fascinating, ever-shifting reflection of atmospheric conditions. The subtle design behind each of Nakaya's fog installations is determined by their interplay with site-specific microclimates. Using readings taken by an anemometer, a device employed by meteorologists to measure wind velocity and here located on the roof of Pier 17, Nakaya has designed the installation at the Exploratorium to respond to weather data updated at ten minute intervals. Working in tandem with fluctuating wind speeds, a computer program modulates the release of high-pressured water through hundreds of tiny nozzles lining the footbridge connecting Piers 15 and 17. A tiny pin in each nozzle atomizes the water into microscopic droplets creating a fine vapor, or fog.

The sensitive technology enabling *Fog Bridge* allows the work to highlight dramatic and subtle shifts in weather. Given San Francisco's changeable weather conditions, the experience of *Fog Bridge* varies dramatically day by day, even hour by hour. On warm, still days the fog billows and envelops the bridge before dissipating over the water in delicate, wispy veils. On wet, gray days the fog builds up into denser, more stable, pillows of moisture. On extremely windy days the fog dramatically fills the canyon between Piers 15 and 17 with long streams of vapor flowing east towards the Exploratorium's Observatory or west towards the Embarcadero. Nakaya's installation provides a heightened experience of fog in every weather condition, compelling us to notice its ever-changing forms and the otherwise invisible movements of the wind.

Photograph of an "imperfect" snow crystal by Dr. Ukichiro Nakaya, 1930s. Image courtesy of Fujiko Nakaya

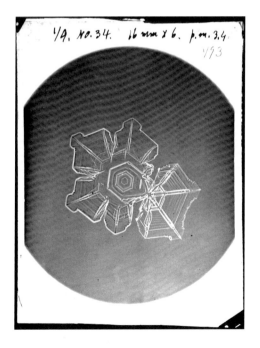

Ned Kahn
developing *Tornado*.
Photo: Susan
Schwartzenberg,
ca. 1985
© Exploratorium

Observation has been an important aspect of the artistic inquiries
promoted by the Exploratorium for more than four decades. One of
the Exploratorium's first artistic projects was the installation *Sun
Painting* created by former staff artist, scientist, and educator Bob
Miller in 1973 and now on view in the Central Gallery.[4] This work
uses a heliostat located on the roof of the building to track the sun's
movement in the sky. A series of mirrors conduct the sunlight into the
museum where it is funneled through prisms, refracted into a bright
spectrum of colors, and reflected dramatically onto a wall.

In 1983 Exploratorium staff artist Ned Kahn began emulating natural phenomena in works such as *Tornado* (1990), which remarkably
models the dynamics of an actual tornado.[5] Kahn has also artificially
generated fog for his exhibits and has developed many projects that
allow us to perceive wind patterns. Inspired by "atmospheric physics, geology, astronomy and fluid motion," Kahn's works recreate the
complex systems found in nature in order to intensify our observation of natural phenomena.[6] In 1997 former Exploratorium Arts
Director Peter Richards, in collaboration with research physicist Jim

Charles Sowers
*Watch Water
Freeze* (detail).
Photo: Amy
Snyder, 2001
© Exploratorium

Crutchfield, an expert in the new field of complexity studies, curated the exhibition *Turbulent Landscapes* featuring a large collection of Kahn's work. The exhibition also included *Spring Box* (1997), an early work by Exploratorium staff artist Shawn Lani. Lani, along with fellow staff artist Charles Sowers and artist-in-residence Michael Brown—all of whom were mentored and inspired by Kahn—has since created arresting museum exhibits evoking the beauty and delight of ice, geysers, wind, fog, water, and bubbles.

This strand of the Exploratorium's exhibit development practice has evolved over the years in step with new approaches in culture and science. Originally works and displays took the form of tabletop-scale experiments informed by the methods used by research physicists in a laboratory setting. More recently this aspect of the museum's work has drawn upon the combined tools and methodologies of the observational sciences, as well as urban history and geography, and expanded in scale to include whole landscapes.[7] For the re-opening of the Exploratorium at Pier 15 Lani, who now directs the Exploratorium Outdoor Studio, biologist Kristina Yu, who oversees Life Sciences, and staff artist Susan Schwartzenberg, have directed the work of multidisciplinary teams comprised of artists, engineers, ecologists, urban geographers, microbiologists, cartographers, astronomers, and filmmakers in the creation of East Gallery, the Exploratorium's first Outdoor Gallery, and the glass-enclosed Bay Observatory Gallery.[8] Collaborators include artists Amy Balkin and John Roloff; filmmaker Sam Green; and filmmaker, archivist, and writing duo Rick and Megan Prelinger, amongst many others. Together they have created a complex, layered picture of the place where we live and the dynamic systems through which it is continually reshaped. These exhibits, in dialog with Nakaya's *Fog Bridge*, allow us to understand fog in relation to Bay Area geography, weather systems, ocean currents, water cycles, and seasons.

The radical experimentation of the 1960s that inspired the Exploratorium also shaped Nakaya's artistic sensibilities. Her path to becoming a fog artist originated over forty years ago in a project that valued the kind of cross-disciplinary collaboration the Museum espouses.[9] In 1968 Nakaya began working with the seminal group Experiments in Art and Technology (E.A.T.). Founded in 1966 with a mission to "develop collaboration between groups unrealistically developing in isolation," E.A.T. was born in a pre-Internet era when access to technology, knowledge, and expertise across fields was more limited. The operation seeded collaborations between artists and engineers and brought together many talents. E.A.T. was "an open-ended experiment" driven by the passion of core members who evolved to include Bell Labs engineers Billy Klüver and Fred Waldhauer, artist Robert Rauschenberg, sound artist David Tudor, and performance artist/filmmaker Robert Whitman.[10]

Nakaya met Rauschenberg and Tudor when they travelled to Tokyo in 1964 with the Merce Cunningham Dance Company, and first became involved with E.A.T. in 1968 through their Pepsi Pavilion project for the Osaka '70 Expo. Eventually, Nakaya went on to direct E.A.T.'s Tokyo office.

The Pepsi Pavilion was a domed structure designed by the Japanese construction company Takenaka Komuten. The E.A.T. artists, however, did not care for its design and so they proposed an aesthetic strategy to transform it. According to Nakaya:

> The core artists decided to shroud the Pavilion with an artificial cloud. They all agreed that the roof . . . looked like a fake Fuller Dome and was so ugly that it should be hidden by a cloud. They called it the 'Buckled Fuller Dome' in a pun on Fuller's name.[11]

Nakaya had already been thinking of creating an artwork informed by temperature differences and volunteered to help with the research. When Klüver discovered her many Japanese connections in the field of meteorology, due primarily to her father, he asked Nakaya to oversee the project.

For her research, Nakaya studied the atmospheric conditions that produce fog and explored the various techniques available for creating fog artificially. Technically defined as low-lying clouds that obscure visibility, fog, like snow, forms on small particles called cloud condensation nuclei. These particles can be made of dust, soot, sea salt, or other tiny airborne elements. When air cools, relative humidity increases and water molecules in the atmosphere condense onto these small particles. Fog can be artificially generated by seeding nuclei chemically, but Nakaya was convinced of the necessity of inventing a water-based technique in order to create a more people-friendly environment for the E.A.T. Pavilion.

When, after much research and testing, Nakaya eventually exhausted the potential of Japanese technology to achieve her aims, Klüver put her in touch with the Pasadena-based cloud physicist Thomas Mee. A former Cornell University research scientist, Mee had started a small company in his family's Altadena garage to manufacture and sell high-tech weather instruments in 1969. Though he had at one time experimented with the production of water-based fog, Mee eventually came to rely on ammonia and chloride to chemically produce fog in conjunction with frost prevention in fruit orchards.[12] Nakaya, however, persuaded Mee to return to his earlier research.

Their numerous conversations, her frequent visits to California, and Mee's backyard experimentation eventually yielded results in the form of the first water-generated fog.[13] To this day, a configuration of pumps capable of compressing water at very high pressure forces water through copper water lines dotted with nozzles. The nozzles have openings as small as 160 microns, or six-thousandths of an inch, in diameter and are fitted with microscopically sized pins that atomize the water into billions of ultra-fine fog droplets measuring between fifteen and twenty microns in diameter.

The first demonstration of water fog by cloud physicist Thomas Mee in the backyard of his house in Altadena, California, August 1969. Image courtesy Mee Industries, Inc.

Pepsi Pavilion, 1970. Exterior: Fujiko Nakaya *Fog Sculpture #47773*. Interior: *Mirror Dome*, design concept by Bob Whitman and Robert Breer with Billy Klüver. Expo '70, Osaka, Japan. Photos: Fujiko Nakaya

The water-based fog successfully covered the Pepsi Pavilion and led to a forty-year collaboration between Nakaya and Mee Industries. Their work remains a potent example of the innovation that can result when artists and engineers work together. Today Mee Industries is run by Mee's son Thomas and his daughter D'Arcy and uses the same water-based fog technology for agricultural and industrial applications including the cooling of greenhouses, data centers, and gas turbines in power plants.

16

Creating an open-ended experience that allows the participant freedom to explore has been an important aspect of Nakaya's fog installations. For the Pepsi Pavilion, Nakaya and her E.A.T. collaborators[14] sought to create an environment that placed the visitor at the center of an immersive, self-directed experience.[15] According to Nakaya, the same participatory ideal that animated the founding vision for the Exploratorium informed mee the design of the Pavilion:

> The concept was to do away with the binary relationships between showing and being shown for a live environment of sound and image where people could explore and create their own experiences. The empty space would respond to the participation of the visitor and transform itself in myriad ways. . . it was a time when artists had discovered the importance of environment and the value of interrelated experiences. The word 'environment' at that time held the promise of recovering certain sensibilities and human values through cultivating awareness of the mutually influential nature relationships between individuals and the outside world. It goes without saying that the term has come to include a more acute and complex range of meanings today.[16]

Nakaya's Osaka environment was based on the provision of an aesthetic experience of "fog to walk in, to feel and smell, and disappear in."[17] Continuing in that vein, *Fog Bridge* affords ample room for play and improvisation: for getting wet, for hiding in dense vapors, or for standing at a distance and observing the movement of fog and its effect on the surrounding space.

As Henry Urbach describes later in this catalog, an important feature of fog is its ability to obscure visibility and change our perception of surrounding space. Thomas Mee outlined the technical reasons behind fog's effect on our visual perception as follows:

> The droplets or particles have diameters 10–20 times the wavelength of green light, which causes the mass of particles to appear as a white hazy substance. This is because the human eye cannot distinguish the individual particles and sees only the scattered light that has bounced many, many times from one particle to another.[18]

Perhaps this effect of fog on our vision explains its maligned associations in Western culture. We associate fog with murkiness and obfuscation, with "foggy thinking." And yet, the fog of Nakaya's *Fog Bridge* makes it possible for us to see the otherwise invisible dynamics of the atmosphere.

Though it may initially seem curious to engineer fog in San Francisco, Nakaya's *Fog Bridge* is a study and revelation of the power of observation. Her own artistic inquiry into weather may just become infectious, leading us to love fog even on a warm summer's day.

1   Harold Gilliam, *Weather of the San Francisco Bay Region* (Berkeley: University of California Press, 2002), 1.

2   Ukichiro Nakaya's richly illustrated book *Snow Crystals: Natural and Artificial* (Boston: Harvard University Press, 1954), remains an important reference for the field of snow studies. His first film, *Snow Crystals*, was made in 1939.

Nakaya also conducted some of the first ice-coring experiments in Greenland and wrote about the potential for anthropogenic climate change as early as 1957 in an essay entitled "Moon World in White." Fujiko Nakaya oversees her father's archive to this day and has organized numerous exhibitions of his work including *Conversations With Snow and Ice* at the Natural History Museum of Latvia (November 10, 2005–January 8, 2006).

3   Ukichiro Nakaya realized that earlier classification systems excluded asymmetrical or "imperfect" snow crystals as well as their three-dimensional aspects. Snow crystals take shape slowly as they fall through the atmosphere, growing on small airborne particles called nuclei. The Nakaya Diagram is based on the observation that different kinds of crystals form at different temperatures and levels of humidity. Nakaya became interested in growing snowflakes artificially in order to better study this formation; his challenge was to find a material conducive to ice nucleation. Working in a room resembling a walk-in freezer at the Low Temperature Science Laboratory, which Nakaya directed at Hokkaido University, the scientist and his students discovered that the nodules of the rabbit-hair lining their parka jackets were ideal for ice nucleation, and thus the growing of artificial snow crystals.

4   Bob Miller is also celebrated for his *Image Walks*, which transformed the way in which we notice and understand the dappled, reflected, and refracted rays of everyday sunlight. See http://www.exploratorium.edu/sln/light_walk/ Accessed February 10, 2013.

5   Kahn worked at the Exploratorium for thirteen years and has since developed large-scale public projects as an independent artist. For *Tornado* (1990) fans situated below a tall, walk-in, glass volume, shape airflow patterns that are made visible by water vapor released into the top of the structure.

6   From the artist statement at http://nedkahn.com. Accessed December 22, 2012.

7   The prototype for the Outdoor Gallery at Pier 15 was The Outdoor Exploratorium at Fort Mason, which was funded by a grant from the National Science Foundation. Peter Richards was the principal investigator, and Shawn Lani the lead exhibit developer, for the project, which was realized in partnership with the Golden Gate National Recreational

Area and the Fort Mason Center. The project debuted in 2010 and included twenty outdoor exhibits. See http://www.exploratorium.edu/outdoor/#/vrlocation/you-are-here/. Accessed March 4, 2013.

8   The work of the Bay Observatory Gallery grows out of ten years of research and development initiated by Peter Richards and Susan Schwartzenberg for the project *Invisible Dynamics* sponsored by the National Endowment for the Arts in 2003, and the Andy Warhol Foundation in 2007. *Invisible Dynamics* was included in the ZERO1 Biennial in San Jose in 2006. *Invisible Dynamics* as well as the exhibition *Observing* at the Exploratorium in 2009 presented many prototypes, which have subsequently been further developed for display at Pier 15.

9   Frank Oppenheimer invited the San Francisco chapter of E.A.T. to conduct sound experiments at the Exploratorium in the early 1970s.

10   See Yoshitomo Morioka's essay "A Loose Communion: The Early Work of E.A.T. and its Contemporary Significance" in the exhibition catalog *E.A.T.—The Story of Experiments in Art and Technology* (Tokyo: NTT Intercommunication Center 2003, 105–19), for a wonderful description of the "open house" ethos that animated E.A.T. Fujiko Nakaya details her history with E.A.T. in the essay "On Exper-

iments in Art and Technology (E.A.T.): Activities in Japan and E.A.T. Tokyo," in the same catalog, 120–32.

11   Ibid., 123.

12   Farmers previously used smoke pots to warm the ground and ward off frost.

13   Both Nakaya and Mee later registered patents related to their invention. While Nakaya's patent protects the method of controlling airflow, Mee's protects the design of the hardware and nozzles.

14   Programming for the exterior of the Pepsi Pavilion was designed by Frosty Meyers, Robert Breer, and Nakaya. The interior was designed by Bob Whitman and David Tudor. Billy Klüver oversaw the complete project.

15   See also Billy Klüver's description of E.A.T.'s intentions for visitor experience in *Pavilion*, eds. Billy Klüver, Julie Martin, and Barbara Rose (New York: E.P. Dutton & Co., Inc., 1972), ix.

16   *E.A.T.—The Story of Experiments in Art and Technology*, op. cit., 122.

17   *Pavilion*, op. cit., 207.

18   Ibid., 226.

MARINA MCDOUGALL is Director of the Exploratorium's new Center for Art & Inquiry, a research and development laboratory for the arts within the larger learning laboratory of the Exploratorium. A curator working at the intersections of art, science, nature, and culture, McDougall has twenty years experience organizing exhibitions and public programs. McDougall was the first Curator of Art and Design at the CCA Wattis Institute for Contemporary Art and is a co-founder of the Studio for Urban Projects. She has been a visiting curator at the MIT Media Lab, the Museum of Jurassic Technology, the California Academy of Sciences, and the Oakland Museum of California. McDougall is an Adjunct Professor in the Graduate Program in Curatorial Practice at California College of the Arts.

FUJIKO NAKAYA

Fog Bridge, 2013
Fog Sculpture #72494
832 nozzles, four high pressure pumps, eight feeder water lines, anemometer, Max program

San Francisco Bay fog engulfs "Fog Bridge" –

Fog Sculpture #72494
"FOG BRIDGE"
Over the water
Exploratorium, San Francisco

Fog Bridge

"Fog Bridge" asks Bay fog,
"How may I serve you, master?"

Nature replies,
"...no need. Let's pretend I'm art, too"

Sujibo Nahay   2013

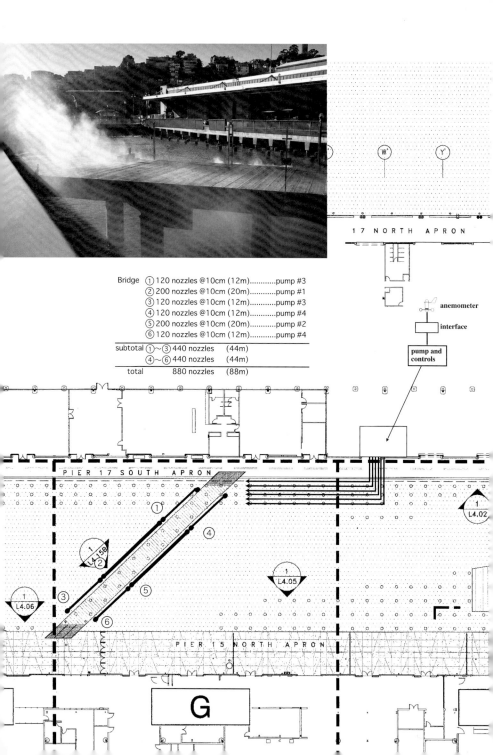

17 NORTH APRON

anemometer

interface

pump and
controls

Bridge ① 120 nozzles @10cm (12m)............pump #3
② 200 nozzles @10cm (20m)............pump #1
③ 120 nozzles @10cm (12m)............pump #3
④ 120 nozzles @10cm (12m)............pump #4
⑤ 200 nozzles @10cm (20m)............pump #2
⑥ 120 nozzles @10cm (12m)............pump #4

subtotal ①~③ 440 nozzles   (44m)
          ④~⑥ 440 nozzles   (44m)
total   880 nozzles   (88m)

PIER 17 SOUTH APRON

①

④

1
L4.15B

②

1
L4.05

③

⑤

1
L4.06

⑥

1
L4.02

PIER 15 NORTH APRON

G

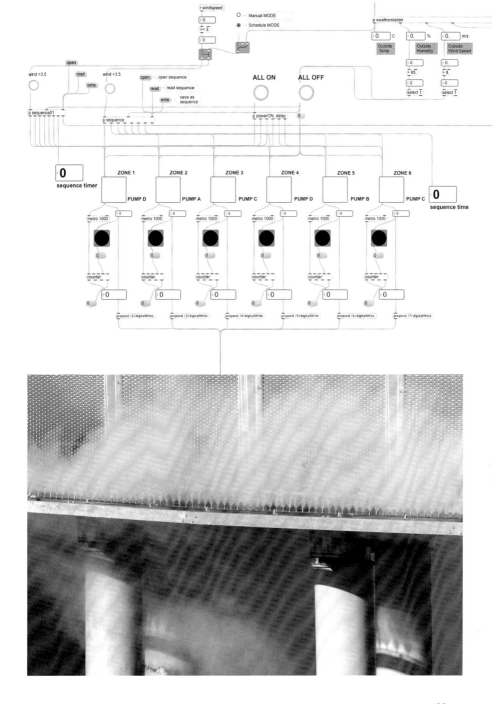

MUTABLE ENVIRONMENTS
Leigh Markopoulos

I like clouds and fog because they are a very sensitive medium to work with. Fog is very responsive to its environment and nature collaborates in creating the work of art. It's not like conventional sculpture, which is a projection of the artist's thoughts into a certain form, carved into wood or formed in metal, which usually has nothing to do with its environment.[1]

By "sculpture" I mean the atmospheric conditions serve as a mold for the wind to carve as it pleases; a mutable environment sculpted from moment to moment, which we can also go inside and experience.[2]

Fog is a readily comprehensible meteorological phenomenon. Its use as an artistic medium may, however, seem perplexing. And yet Fujiko Nakaya's artistic inquiry has for forty years or so centered on the observation of the material and formal properties of water vapor. Since 1970, Nakaya has created numerous site-specific fog installations in cities as far-flung as Sydney, Paris, New York, Bilbao, Shanghai, Toronto, and Riga, and all over Japan. Her fogs have cascaded over, shrouded, and alternately revealed and concealed a mixture of man-made and natural sites from deserts, parks, terraced hills, rivers, museum courtyards, to tumuli. Her installations have ranged in size and intensity from humanly-scaled fog banks generated by ten nozzles to those with more ambitious proportions generated by 2,000 nozzles. She has collaborated with choreographers (Trisha Brown), musicians (David Tudor), artists (Bill Viola, Robert Wilson, Hiroshi Teshigawara) and architects (Diller + Scofidio, Shoei Yoh, Arata Isozaki) to lend her fog to sound, music, and dance creations.

Existing somewhere between "experience-oriented" sculpture,[3] environment, and performance, Nakaya's fog works evince characteristics of Systems and Process art, as well as of other conceptual practices that emerged internationally in the 1960s. More recently, they can be

Fujiko Nakaya
Square Fog #1,
1981. *Fog Sculpture
#47590*. The
Miyagi Museum
of Art, Sendai,
Japan. Photo:
Fujiko Nakaya

seen as sharing the concerns of contemporary artists who make art out of weather conditions, or even simulate natural phenomena such as rain and lightning.[4] Nakaya remains, however, the only artist to devise (in collaboration with engineer Thomas Mee) the technology and software for generating climate-responsive fog installations. Her works are artificial in so far as they are enabled by technology, but materially they are natural.

Regarded as the life breath of the atmosphere by the ancient Japanese, fog has long been considered an important component of traditional Japanese poetry and landscape painting, and has also played a key role in the work of many Western nineteenth-century paintings and novels, evoking uncanny atmospheres and the sublimely unknown, and symbolizing man's relative insignificance in relation to nature. Situated at the edge of the San Francisco Bay, as part of the Exploratorium's new waterfront site, Nakaya's *Fog Bridge* (2013) is more human in scale and more closely linked to a rational history of experimentation in art, science, and technology. Its location on a publicly accessible footbridge announces a public experience and invites interaction.

The changing configurations of visitors are as much of interest to Nakaya as the more existential notions of flux that her works both

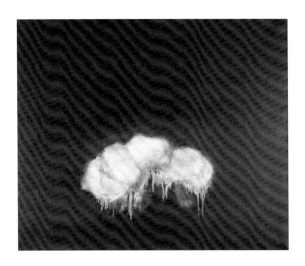

Fujiko Nakaya
Cloud Series,
1964.
Oil on canvas,
15 x 18 inches.
Image courtesy
of the artist

symbolize and manifest. Making visible complex patterns of natural energy exchange, her fog sculptures derive their specificity from a matrix of topographical and meteorological conditions. Nakaya's research into the weather conditions of a particular site is thus key to the development of her projects. Indeed, each work bears the code number of the international weather station where it is, or was, sited (in San Francisco's case #72494). Wind is particularly important to her calculations, but her expressed interest is "less in how to control the wind than in how to negotiate with it."[5] In this negotiation, Nakaya views her role as being "to design a landscape that interacts with the wind, to create a stage where the fog can perform," and she has often stressed her collaborative approach toward the environment.[6] New media historian Anne-Marie Duguet has written the following about the artist's approach to location:

> Whether man-made or natural, the venue is examined for its ability to provoke or constrain forms, becoming an active parameter in the work. Where necessary, Nakaya will actually invent the landscape—assist it, so to speak—by adding obstacles such as a hedge to block the wind . . . . Thus she (re)lays the groundwork for the introduction of a phenomenon that will radically change our perception of landscape.[7]

The architecture supporting *Fog Bridge*, however, remains unaltered and exposed to the elements. In tandem with San Francisco's capricious weather—rapidly fluctuating wind, temperature, and moisture levels—this work will constantly transform, radically altering our perception of climatic activity.

While it is important to consider Nakaya's cultural and familial (her father Ukichiro Nakaya was a pioneering scientist) heritage in her artistic formation, it is helpful also to consider her formal training

28

and the artistic milieu in which she developed her fog sculptures. Nakaya's career as an artist began in a fairly conventional way. Following a high school education in Tokyo she attended Northwestern University in Evanston, Illinois, where she majored in art in 1957. Nakaya then continued her studies in Europe, studying painting in the museums of Paris and Madrid until 1959. In 1960 her oil paintings were the subject of a two-person exhibition at Devorah Sherman Gallery, Chicago. She returned to Japan that same year and in 1962 presented twelve paintings in her first solo exhibition, at the Tokyo Gallery.

Nakaya's subjects were from the beginning nature and the cycle of life. She painted trees, landscapes, and coral reefs rejecting representation in favor of a dynamic, expressionistic style. In this regard Nakaya's impulse was aligned with the various schools of Action painting that were operating at the time. Although not affiliated with

Shozo Shimamoto hurling paint-filled bottles at canvases, n.d., (late 1950s/ early 1960s). Image courtesy of Shimamoto Lab, Nishinomiya, Japan

the Japanese collective Gutai Art Association, she shared their emphasis on the process of making and their blurring of the distinction between creative and destructive acts. Gutai co-founder Shozo Shimamoto, for example, made paintings by smashing bottles of paint against the canvas or concrete. Taking a less drastic approach, Nakaya's technique was yet often performative: she used her fingers to apply and position paint and, later, a turpentine-soaked rag to effect its partial removal. While she initially layered paint to complicate her

E.A.T. Tokyo
Utopia Q&A 1981,
1971. "Xerox Knowl-
edge-In" sculpture.
From left E.A.T.
Tokyo members
Hakudo Kobayashi,
Fujiko Nakaya,
and Yuji Morioka.
Sony Building, Ginza,
Tokyo, Japan.
Photo: E.A.T. Tokyo

compositions, in her later paintings she experimented with partially removing the impastoed layers (with turpentine) in order to compose through, in her words, "de-composition." Resisting the notion of composition central to classical painting, she sought instead to imbue her canvases with an elemental dynamism. Her paintings can thus be seen as attempts to incorporate a sense of duration and development, rather than to arrest a particular moment.

Ultimately, however, paint proved too resistant a medium for her ends and Nakaya became increasingly interested in a direct engagement with more ephemeral materials. A series of paintings about the ocean led her to consider harnessing the actual processes of water condensation and evaporation to make artificial clouds and fog:

> I started thinking about working with temperature difference, which is responsible for changes in a lot of forms of nature—in animals and in people and things. I made dry-ice clouds on a plate with a heater underneath. So I was experimenting with the change of form through temperature difference.[8]

Her investigations into thermodynamics were paralleled by those of other artists interested in investigating phenomena more often considered the domain of science and technology at a time in which the categories of acceptable artistic media were radically redefined.

Characterized by experimentation and change, the 1960s saw rapid developments and new discoveries in the fields of medicine, aeronautics, computing, and other forms of technology. A utopian faith in progress inspired a number of artists to make work that addressed specifically the potential of technology. A number of curators labeled their concerns as Kinetic, Systems, and Process art, presenting them in exhibitions such *Dylaby* (1961), *Primary Structures* (1962), *The Machine as Seen at the End of the Mechanical Age* (1968), *Systems* (1969), and *Information* (1970). And a number of institutions initiated art and technology programs. The Los Angeles County Museum of Art (LACMA), for instance, launched theirs in 1967 under the stewardship of curator Maurice Tuchman. This four-year endeavor placed artists representing the spectrum of artistic production at the time—from Robert Irwin and James Turrell to Oyvind Fahlstrom, Andy Warhol, and Jackson MacLow—in residence in leading technological and industrial corporations in California and beyond. Tuchman, writing in the introduction to the marvelously transparent report issued by LACMA about the program, noted that:

> International developments in art have provided the impetus for this project: much of the most compelling art since 1910 has depended upon the materials and processes of technology, and has increasingly assimilated scientific and industrial advances.[9]

Indeed, the Exploratorium itself was founded by the physicist Frank Oppenheimer in recognition of these "advances," and the importance of the public having the opportunity to learn about their broader implications. The Museum's doors officially opened in November 1969 with *Cybernetic Serendipity*—a travelling exhibition dedicated to the potential and actual relationships between computers and the arts.

Happily, Nakaya's scientific interests brought her into the orbit of Experiments in Art and Technology (E.A.T.) in the late 60s. A loose association of artists and engineers, formalized in 1966 by Bell Telephone Laboratories research engineer Billy Klüver and artist Robert Rauschenberg to facilitate collaborative projects, E.A.T. espoused a "more humanized version of technology."[10] They were not alone in their efforts. The Massachusetts Institute of Technology (MIT) and its research exhibiting arms, as well as the related (and still operational) Center of Advanced Visual Studies (CAVS) also sought to promote this very specific interdisciplinary cross-pollination. Believing in the social role of the artist, MIT Professor Gyorgy Kepes conceived of CAVS as a fellowship program for artists. With the founding of CAVS, he sought to bring about the:

Absorption of the new technology as an artistic medium; the interaction of artists, scientists, engineers, and industry; the raising of the scale of work to the scale of the urban setting; media geared to all sensory modalities incorporation of natural processes, such as cloud play, water flow, and the cyclical variations of light and weather; [and] acceptance of the participation of 'spectators' in such a way that art becomes a confluence.[11]

A long and international list of Fellows has in the intervening years continued to realize a number of civic and artistic projects, events, and exhibitions informed by Kepes' vision.

In recognition of her work at this same interface, Nakaya was appointed the Tokyo representative of E.A.T. in 1969 and, as has been well documented in *Pavilion* as well as elsewhere in this publication,[12] it was this collaboration that coalesced her artistic and scientific endeavors. More specifically, the commission to shroud the unsightly Pepsi Pavilion's domed exterior in fog during the 1970 Expo in Osaka catalyzed her collaboration with Thomas Mee, a West Coast based engineer. Inspired by Nakaya's desire to create a purely water-based fog, Mee invented a type of nozzle that could funnel and disperse minute drops of water in such a way as to provoke an authentic layer of mist. The technology was successfully deployed in creating a fog-blanket for the Pavilion's exterior and simultaneously launched Nakaya on her career.

While Nakaya's scientific impetus in single-mindedly pursuing the effects of fog seems clear, her work can also be seen as challenging

Robert Morris
STEAM,
1974 refabrication
of a 1967 original.
Steam, multiple
steam outlets under
a bed of stones,
outlined with wood.
Dimensions variable.
Installation view at
Western Washington
University, Belling-
ham. © 2013 Robert
Morris/Artists Rights
Society (ARS), New
York. Image courtesy
of the Sonnabend
Gallery, New York

the tenets of Minimalism, which had dominated artistic production, and in particular sculpture, for the earlier part of the decade. The proposition that the art object was autonomous and should consist solely of form and material had seemed radical at the beginning of the sixties. But the emergence of a more self- and socially-aware artistic practice at the end of the decade privileged instead the questioning of the relationship between a work of art and its various environments. The form of sculpture (weighty, solid) and the role of the artist (divorced from reality) were challenged and reinvented. Natural processes formed the medium and subject of many artists from the Light and Space group in Los Angeles, to the proponents of Arte Povera in Italy, and conceptual artists like Robert Barry and his experiments with inert gases. Turning their backs on the industrial materials of Minimalism—lead, steel, and copper—artists courted ephemeral media, often to create semblances of natural phenomena. David Medalla's "cloud sculptures," for example, were generated by soap-bubble machines, which by spilling their foamy product into the gallery space created a hypnotic cascade of changing forms. Robert Morris steam sculptures were the product of concealed humidifiers and simulated subterranean thermal activity when situated in nature.

This pursuit of unstable media more closely allied to the natural than artistic world in the service of process-oriented explorations

Hans Haacke
Condensation Cube,
1963–65.
Plexiglas and
water. 30 x 30 x 30
inches. © Hans
Haacke / Artists
Rights Society
(ARS), New York /
VG Bild-Kunst, Bonn
Image courtesy
of the artist

was analyzed by critics such as Lucy Lippard in her book *Six Years: The Dematerialization of the Art Object 1966–72*, and Rosalind Krauss in essays such as "Sculpture in the Expanded Field." Artist and writer Jack Burnham considered additionally the turn toward science and technology in this trajectory under the heading "systems aesthetics." In two key articles published in *Artforum*—"Systems Esthetic" (1968) and "Real Time Systems" (1969)—Burnham appraised artistic responses to new technologies manifest, for example, in early computer and video art. He noted also that this artistic turn toward systems thinking reflected a general interest in biological and cybernetic research, and open systems and communication networks (as expounded in the writings of Ludwig von Bertalanffy, Ervin László, Claude Shannon, and Norbert Wiener amongst others), as well as cross-fertilization between these different areas of inquiry.

Burnham's conclusions are supported by Nakaya's fog sculptures, but also by her extended practice, which in the early seventies included experimental video art, and what could be seen as an early, and prescient, example of social practice art, *Utopia Q&A 1981* (1971).[13] The first collective and international endeavor of E.A.T. Tokyo, this project was staged simultaneously in Tokyo, New York, Stockholm, and Ahmedabad, India. Participants in each city were encouraged to communicate with their counterparts abroad by using the (free) Telex lines provided as part of the installation, and conversations were initiated by speculative propositions about the year 1981, a decade into the future. A precursor, in a way, to the social media of the Internet, the project promoted a network of global communication between individuals.

A close friend and sometime collaborator of Burnham's, artist Hans Haacke initially made works that perhaps most clearly parallel Nakaya's inquiry, "captur[ing] "natural" systems for art with an elegant minimum of technology, in order to . . . contemplate non-human agency."[14] Haacke's *Condensation Cube* (1963–65), for example, comprises a transparent Plexiglas cube into which the introduction of water is facilitated by a tiny hole in a corner of the upper surface. Enclosed in the cube, the water reacts to temperature variations by alternately evaporating and condensing. The cycle generates an endless array of unpredictable, constantly varying patterns of droplets and watery trails on the Plexiglas walls. Nakaya's fragile natural systems offer equally little by way of imposed composition—changes are desired and courted; form is provided by a constellation of site-specific meteorological and topographical conditions.

In *Condensation Cube* and other early works such as *Wave* (1964), *Ice Stick* (1966), and *Wide White Flow* (1967), Haacke explored the notion of "non-human agency" by making use of the natural physics of water and wind processes to display:

> A physical process, which, in principle, occurs independently of the viewer. In opposition to the universality of the here and now, Haacke [sets in motion] a temporal chain conditioned by external circumstances and based on transformation.[15]

Poised between tangible art object and the invisible realm of concept, his works, like Nakaya's, privileged a human subject as a perceiver of, or participant in, a system that excludes him/her, albeit for different reasons. In so doing, both artists sought to unsettle viewers' habitual ways of seeing and comprehending. Nakaya, "[wanted] people to get out of their stereotyped reactions to the environment and experience it in a different way."[16]

By engaging audiences physically and perceptually with her fog works, she continues to promote a dialogue with the natural environment, emphasizing the value of individual contemplation as much as of social participation.

In the intervening forty or so years since the experimentation of the sixties and the Pepsi Pavilion breakthrough, many other artists have replicated, or are using, atmospheric conditions of one sort or another as part of their practice, and to many different effects. Of particular interest in this context are the Light and Space artists who were working in and around LA predominantly in the late 60s and 70s. Robert Irwin, for example, has created numerous installations in which natural light—often filtered through transparent scrims—is used to define space. His subtly evolving environments intensify sensory awareness and heighten the experience of light at the same time as they enact a form of critique on more traditional art forms by casting light as a medium. James Turrell's immersive color environments have since the 80s been supplemented by a series of installations, which are more closely related to Nakaya's project. Entitled "skyspaces," they comprise simple cell-like rooms, their ceilings partially or wholly removed, their walls more often than not painted white. Directing the viewer's gaze upward, the bare walls frame the sky, focusing attention on the advancing or fading light of day, often with spectacular effect. This particular series of works echoes Nakaya's desire to encourage the process of conscious perception—viewers should really look, and see. In addition, Light and Space artworks have frequently—and aptly—inspired both scientific and metaphysical interpretations. Nakaya's fogscapes, too, conjure the transcendental, and she has often credited the influence of Buddhist-Shinto philosophy, especially with regard to the notions of change and renewal evoked by the cycle of water evanescing into fog and back into water in the atmosphere.

The artist perhaps most readily associated with the introduction of weather phenomena into the confines of the gallery space is Danish-Icelandic artist, Olafur Eliasson. A significant aspect of his multi-faceted practice involves creating an architectural feature out of meteorology. Whether this takes the form of an indoor rainbow glistening on curtains of falling water (*Beauty*, 1993), or a giant setting sun in Tate Modern's Turbine Hall (*The Weather Project*, 2003), Eliasson is less concerned with mimicking or proposing an illusion (the technological props he uses are often visible) and more with encouraging a moment

Olafur Eliasson
*The weather
project*, 2003.
Installation.
Turbine Hall, Tate
Modern, London.
Photo: Studio
Olafur Eliasson
© Olafur Eliasson,
2013

of reflection and pause, an orchestrated confrontation with natural phenomena in cultural environments from which they are usually excluded.

Belgian artist Ann Veronica Janssens' practice focuses more directly on perception and she often uses artificial fog to create situations, which in obstructing perception enhance the functions of other human senses, such as smell and touch. Filling an enclosed gallery space or a specially manufactured Plexiglas chambers with fog, and on occasion even siting her installations outdoors, Janssens is interested less in directing one's attention and more in isolating the mechanics of seeing. Her works differ from Nakaya's not only conceptually, but also in their makeup—the fog is generated by dry ice and visitors often comment on the sound of the generators making the fog or its chemical smell.[17] In Janssens' case it is not then the recreation of a natural environment that is at stake, but rather the temporary deprivation of another; the impediment of one sense in order to promote acuity in the others.

That Nakaya's work finds its time in every decade and continues to exist alongside a multitude of different practices is undoubtedly due to our ongoing fascination with fog as a natural phenomenon, but also its recreation as an artwork. Whole histories of sculpture can be read into Nakaya's fogscapes. The relationship between the static elements of landscape or architecture and the constantly regenerating, aleatory architecture of the fog itself is at heart a poetic critique of the fundamental nature of sculpture. In choosing a medium that effectively decomposes as it is created, the stability of the work is undermined, or at least our expectations about such a work, and the validity of the concepts of solidity and permanence are brought

Ann Veronica Janssens, *Blue, red and yellow*, 2001. 11.4 x 29.5 x 14.75 feet. Neuenationalgalerie, Berlin. Image courtesy of the artist

into question. Nakaya's work is thereby safeguarded from becoming entangled in the snares of representation. One can return repeatedly to her fog installations in order to see them in a different context, to reinterpret them, or to understand them anew. They are neither hermetic nor self-referential, but require the viewer's active participation. They provoke and entertain, raise deep theoretical and existential issues, as much as enchant with their playfulness. In recent years we have expanded definitions of art to encompass "environment," or a place for experience, and it is this that Nakaya's fogscapes perhaps most clearly continue to offer.

1   "Island Eye Island Ear: Fujiko Nakaya interviewed by Billy Klüver" in *Fog/Brouillard* (Paris: éditions Anarchive, 2012), 112.

2   Fujiko Nakaya, "From Means to Method: 'Form of Zen Observed in Video,'" ibid., 346.

3   "Island Eye Island Ear," op cit., 114.

4   *Scattered Showers – Forms of Weather*, an exhibition currently (March 8–May 19, 2013) on view at the Frankfurter Kunstverein, Germany, brings together artists whose work is centrally concerned with different forms of weather, exploring not only the physical and aesthetical properties of various meteorological manifestations, but also their political and psychological implications.

5   "Conversations with the Wind: Fujiko Nakaya interviewed by Julie Martin," in *Fog/Brouillard*, op. cit., 229.

6   Ibid.

7   Anne-Marie Duguet, "Naturally Artificial," in *Fog/Brouillard*, op cit., 34.

8   "Island Eye Island Ear," op.cit., 114.

9   Maurice Tuchman, *A Report on the Art and Technology Program of the Los Angeles County Museum of Art, 1967–71*, (New York: Viking, 1971), 11.

10   "From Means to Method: 'Form of Zen Observed in Video,'" op.cit., 346.

11   Gyorgy Kepes, Massachusetts Institute of Technology, The Center for Advanced Visual Studies, introductory brochure on the Center (Cambridge, Mass.: MIT, 1968), n.p., quoted in Elizabeth Finch, "A Brief History of the Center for Advanced Visual Studies, Massachusetts Institute of Technology," http://cavs.mit.edu/about/id.3.html.

12   Experiments in Art and Technology, *Pavilion*, eds. Billy Kluver, Julie Martin, and Barbara Rose (New York: E.P. Dutton & Co., Inc., 1972).

13   Nakaya is considered an important figure in Japan's video art history. In 1972 she founded VIDEO HIROBA with Katsuhiro Yamaguchi, Yoshiaki Tono, Nobuhiro Kawanaka, Hakudo Kobayashi, and others. The aim of the group was to break through the established notion of art and explore video as a process and means of communication. In 1979 Nakaya established Processart Inc. to distribute artists' video works.

14   Caroline A. Jones, "Hans Haacke 1967," *Hans Haacke 1967*, exh. cat. (Cambridge: MIT List Visual Arts Center, 2008), 7.

15   Jenny Schlezker, "More Than One Sees," *Political/Minimal*, exh. cat. (Berlin: Kunst Werke, 2008), 23.

16   "Island Eye Island Ear," op.cit., 112.

17   Stella Brennan, "Ann Veronica Janssens: This Very Shining Moment," http://stella.net.nz/text-by-ann-veronica-janssens/. Accessed January 1, 2013.

LEIGH MARKOPOULOS is the chair of the Graduate Program in Curatorial Practice at the California College of the Arts. Formerly the director of Rena Bransten Gallery, Markopoulos came to San Francisco to take up the position of deputy director of the CCA Wattis Institute for Contemporary Arts. Prior to that she was exhibition organizer at London's Serpentine Gallery and Hayward Gallery. She has organized over fifty exhibitions ranging from solo shows of Richard Artschwager, Briget Riley, and Brice Marden to major group exhibitions such as *Monuments for the USA* and *IRREDUCIBLE: Contemporary Short Form Video*. Markopoulos has contributed numerous reviews and essays on the subjects of curating and contemporary art.

The author would particularly like to thank Studio Eliasson, Hans Haacke, Ann Veronica Janssens, Andrea Mardegan, Xan Price, Heidi Rabben, and Ming Tiampo for their help with sourcing and supplying images.

DISAPPEARING ACTS: THE FOGSCAPES OF FUJIKO NAKAYA
Henry Urbach

The interplay of weather and architecture is complex and multi-faceted, the former offering a steady, if unpredictable, counterpoint to the propositions of the built world. Fog, in particular, has the capacity to temporarily transform places by thickening space in ways that draw things in and out of visibility. In a place such as San Francisco, where fog is frequent and mighty, this interplay can be extremely dramatic as buildings, and even large parts of the city, regularly disappear from view.

Enter the installations of Fujiko Nakaya, works that reproduce fog, its atmospheric effects, and its capacity to alter the appearance of the surrounding environment. By channeling water through nozzles at extremely high pressure, Nakaya is able to create extraordinary scenes of mist and fog that range from cloud-like immersive environments to more figural elements, such as cascades, and projects that function as veils or drapery for buildings and landscapes. Her fifty or so fogscapes, created over the last four decades, may be considered a form of spatial practice, one that is concerned with the production of atmospheres that are dense, dynamic, participatory, and transformative.

Consider, for example, *Fog Bridge* (2013), a project commissioned by the San Francisco Exploratorium, for which Nakaya has covered a footbridge in fog, inviting visitors to pass through a thick, moving mist. Within this space, a damp chill prevails and vision is hindered; when seen from beyond, as an object, the artificial fog obscured views to the Bay and San Francisco skyline in constantly changing ways. The perceptual effects of the city's fog—including the ways in which it continuously reveals and conceals parts of the urban environment—are reproduced here as a kind of performance.

Nakaya's *Earth Talk* (1976) produced a similar condition on a larger scale in a city where fog is not so prevalent. Here, in an open space opposite Sydney's Art Gallery of New South Wales, Nakaya installed a fog sculpture measuring approximately 50,000 square feet, inviting people to pass in and out of the mist to experience two very different

Fujiko Nakaya
Foggy Forest, 1992.
Fog Environment #47660.
Children's Forest,
Showa Kinen Park,
Tachikawa,
Tokyo, Japan.
Photo: Shigeo Ogawa

spatial conditions. Within the area loosely bounded by this fogscape, near vision was muted; when seen from afar, the fog rising from the ground obscured views of the building beyond, bringing its tectonic features in and out of view.

This kind of obfuscation or neutralization occurs in many of Nakaya's projects, beginning with the fog shroud she engineered for the Pepsi Pavilion at Expo '70 in Osaka. Here her project was part of a collaborative effort to produce an exhibition environment that was immersive, participatory, and multi-sensory. The mist, which could be seen from a great distance across the fairground, combined with changing winds to continually modify viewers' perception of the faceted structure. Nakaya's work in Osaka marked the beginning of a way of making art that is dialogic insofar as the work transforms the appearance of its surroundings. This effect may also be clearly seen in her stunning installation *Foggy Forest* in Showa Memorial Park (1992), in which the ziggurat-like forms that Nakaya molded into the constructed landscape are intermittently occluded by wafting drifts of mist.

Always theatrical, Nakaya's work has sometimes taken an explicit turn toward performance, as seen in her stage sets for Trisha Brown

This is How You will Disappear, 2010. Directed by Gisèle Vienne. Fujiko Nakaya *Fog Performance #07579*. 64th Avignon Festival, Gymnase Aubanel, Avignon, France. Photo: Silveri © DACM

and Bill Viola, among others. One of her collaborations, a project with choreographer Gisèle Vienne for the Avignon Festival, is aptly titled *This is How You Will Disappear* (2010). Fog appeared twice during the performance, swallowing a dancer at one point for eight minutes, the longest span possible to maintain fog on stage by manipulating the convection.

Fog, in Nakaya's hands, is a force of decomposition—a term she applied to some of her early paintings—that is, something that makes other things disappear. In her words, "Fog responds constantly to its own environment, revealing and concealing the features of the environment. Fog makes visible things become invisible and invisible things—like wind—become visible."[1] The drama of Nakaya's work resides in the continuous interplay, the ongoing reversal, between what is visible and what is not. Mist swallows up those who enter its atmosphere while also occluding its built and natural surroundings. Known coordinates vanish to be replaced by a miasma, rich in phenomenological effect, that comes and goes.

Around the same time that Nakaya was experimenting with fog in Osaka, a kindred work took shape in the streets of Vienna. There the newly formed architectural studio COOP HIMMELB(L)AU staged one of their early "actions," a work called *Soft Space* (1970) that involved flooding a street with soap bubbles for a period of about ten minutes. A kind of performance, this work turned spectators into willing participants and offered a radically different, even euphoric, experience of the familiar

Diller + Scofidio
Blur, 2002,
Lake Neuchâtel,
Yverdon-les-Bains,
Switzerland. Photo
© Beat Widmer
Image courtesy
of Diller Scofidio
+ Renfro

streetscape. An earlier project, *Hard Space* (1968), used the heartbeats of three individuals to pace multiple explosions in a large field outside Vienna. In both works, the emphasis was on recreating the immediate environment as a stage for experimental and interactive habitation.

In Nakaya's projects, as in COOP HIMMELB(L)AU's, we comprehend the potential of space to elicit intervention and promote new forms of encounter. The intervention—an interruption to normative spatial conditions and practice—is not only something to look at but also a realm to enter and inhabit; viewers become participants or actors in a shared, and distinctly ludic, scene. Space is aerated to fill itself with new and pleasurable possibilities for collective experience.

An architectural project inspired by the spatial qualities of Nakaya's oeuvre is "Blur," a temporary construction by the New York-based interdisciplinary studio Diller + Scofidio that was installed on Lake Neuchâtel, Switzerland, in 2002. Here, in a project for which Nakaya served as an important consultant, a light, steel scaffolding was fully enveloped by mist to produce what the architects describe as an optical white-out marked by the white noise of pulsating nozzles. Commissioned as an exhibition building by the Swiss National Expo, Blur's conceptual aim was to expose visitors' dependence on vision by rendering its object absent, producing an anti-architectural structure that cedes tectonic presence to reemerge as a low-lying cloud.

The precedents for these projects may be found in various avant-garde practices of the late 1950s through 1970s having to do with

COOP HIMMELB(L)AU
Soft Space, 1970.
Vienna, Austria.
Photo © Gertrud
Wolfschwenger

ephemeral means for defining architectural space. Among the most salient are French artist Yves Klein's proposed "air architectures," ways of constructing space beyond the limits of the visible that utilize roofs made of compressed air and other technical assists to produce habitable microclimates. In addition Klein developed, initially in collaboration with architects Werner Ruhnau and Claude Parent, proposals for interventions using fire and water, such as the fifty-flame wall and massive column of fire exhibited outside Krefeld's Museum Haus Lange in 1961, part of his search to conceptualize spaces that were "immaterial, but emotionally, technically, and functionally practical."[2]

We might think as well of Gordon Matta-Clark and his "anarchitecture," an anti-architecture that was fully architectural and included numerous projects concerned with inserting new voids in existing buildings. The institutional authority of architecture was, in this body of work, challenged by the insertion of contrapuntal spatial figures. An example is *Conical Intersect*, which Matta-Clark presented at the 1975 Paris Biennale. Created at the same time that the Centre Beaubourg was replacing a large area of traditional urban fabric, this work reproduced the action of removal at a more intimate, interior scale, inserting a spiraling cut through adjoining seventeenth-century townhouses to yield a huge conical void. In Matta-Clark's work, decomposition and literal deconstruction were proposed as carriers of entropy, in contrast to the progressive aspirations of Modernist architecture and urban planning of the period.

Space, for Nakaya, is not empty but rather full of potential to envelop, to distort, to conceal, and to provoke. Her fogscapes put forward spatial conditions that hold presence and absence in continuous interplay. The clarity, transparency, and emptiness of space, presumed by so many forms of artistic practice, is here superseded by a vision of space that is highly dense, charged, and atmospheric. It stands in a potent and dialogic relation to form—whether bodies or architectural elements—as it swallows things up, or holds them in a state of temporary uncertainty.

Nakaya's works enact a kind of erasure, making things disappear so as to reemerge transformed. Although present, they also function to remove or subtract, bringing presence and absence to bear equivalently. In 1953, Robert Rauschenberg (Nakaya's later friend and collaborator) erased a drawing that he requested from Willem de Kooning expressly for that purpose. Rauschenberg put the drawing in a gold-leaf frame with a handwritten label that read: "Erased de Kooning Drawing, Robert Rauschenberg, 1953," and, with that, produced a work as generative as it was iconoclastic. Nakaya's fog environments share something in common with Rauschenberg's gesture. Confronting buildings and landscapes, making them vanish while bringing new forms to light, they may be seen as disappearing acts, efforts to make

Yves Klein
Creation of a blasted air roof, 23 April 1959. Pencil on tracing paper, 5 x 8 inches. Courtesy Yves Klein Archives, Paris © 2013 Artists Rights Society (ARS), New York / ADAGP Paris

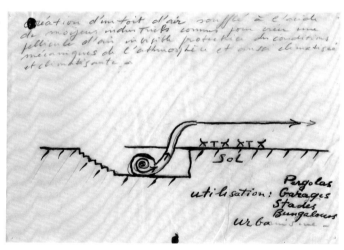

the world of things vanish, if temporarily. By doing so, they bring into being an alternative version of our surroundings, making it possible to see the world, and the contingency of its otherwise certain constructions afresh.

Ultimately, Nakaya's spatial propositions offer a meditation on opacity as a meaningful reaction to the transparency imagined and so widely implemented by Modernism, a kind of interruption in the

Gordon Matta-Clark
Conical Intersect,
1975.
© 2013 Estate
of Gordon Matta
Clark / Artists Rights
Society (ARS),
New York

visual economy that governs so much of contemporary spatial experience. If transparency, and perhaps an attendant sense of certainty, defined the foundations of Modernist architecture and urban form, Nakaya's fogscapes insist on the possibility of a rich spatial counterpoint. Space, in these haunting and evocative works, reemerges as a site of the uncertain, of the not fully-formed, possibly even a site of haunting. By decomposing familiar scenes, and by erasing boundaries of the known, Nakaya invites us to inhabit a disorienting and wondrous zone in which all that is solid melts into not-so-thin air.

1   "Conversations with the Wind,"   2   *INVISIBLE: Art about the Unseen*
Fujiko Nakaya interviewed by Julie   *1957–2012*, exh. cat. (London: Hayward
Martin, in *Fog/Brouillard* (Paris: éditions   Gallery, 2012), 33.
Anarchive, 2012), 229.

HENRY URBACH is director of The Glass House in New Canaan, CT. Home to Philip Johnson and David Whitney until 2005, The Glass House is now a house museum and cultural center that hosts exhibitions, performances, lectures, and other special events. Previously Urbach was curator of architecture and design at the San Francisco Museum of Modern Art, where his exhibitions included Olafur Eliasson's *Your Tempo* (2007) and, in collaboration with Diller Scofidio + Renfro, *How Wine Became Modern: Design + Wine 1976 to Now*." Prior to his time at SFMOMA, Urbach ran a gallery of contemporary art and architecture in New York for nearly ten years. He has written extensively about design, architecture, and culture.

BIOGRAPHY

Fujiko Nakaya was born in Hokkaido, Japan, in 1933. She is the daughter of famed physicist and Hokkaido University professor Ukichiro Nakaya, whose pioneering work in glaciology and low-temperature science led to the creation of the first artificial snow crystal in 1936. After receiving her Bachelor of Arts from Northwestern University, Nakaya studied painting in Europe, eventually returning to Japan in 1960, where she has lived ever since.

In the late 1960s, Nakaya became involved with the newly-formed

Experiments in Art and Technology (E.A.T.) group, founded by Bell Labs engineer Billy Klüver and artist Robert Rauschenberg to encourage daring new collaborative and multidisciplinary work. At Expo '70 in Osaka—a year after she became the Tokyo representative of E.A.T.—she achieved notoriety by creating her first atmospheric sculpture, blanketing the entire exterior of the Pepsi Pavilion in vaporous white fog.

Since then, she has created fog gardens, falls, and geysers around

Fujiko Nakaya
Photo: Gayle Laird, 2012

the world in such locales as the Guggenheim Museum Bilbao (Spain), National Gallery of Australia (Canberra), Jardin de L'Eau (Paris), and the Nakaya Ukichiro Museum of Snow and Ice (Japan). She has collaborated with artists, composers, and dancers such as Trisha Brown, Bill Viola, and David Tudor to develop fog performances and stage sets.

Nakaya is also an accomplished video artist and advocate, establishing Tokyo's first gallery devoted to the viewing, appreciation, and advancement of video-related works, Video Gallery SCAN, in 1980.

As improbable as it may seem, this is Fujiko's first work in San Francisco, a city known the world over for its dramatic fog.

PROCESSART INC. COLLABORATORS

Fujiko Nakaya	artist
Tatsuo Murota	wind specialist (meteorological data analysis)
Sayaka Shimada	production assistant
Shiro Yamamoto	program/interface designer

EXPLORATORIUM *OVER THE WATER* PROJECT TEAM

Kirstin Bach	Program Manager, Center for Art & Inquiry
Eric Diamond	Project Director / Associate Curator Outdoor Works
Steve Gennrich	Senior Project Manager / Engineer, Outdoor Works
Dave Johnson	Exhibit Design Engineer
Shawn Lani	Senior Artist / Curator of Outdoor Works
Herb Masters	Volunteer
Marina McDougall	Director, Center for Art & Inquiry
Thomas Rockwell	Director of Exhibits and Associate Director for Program
Robert Semper, Ph.D.	Executive Associate Director and Director of Program
Jordan Stein	Assistant Curator, Center for Art & Inquiry

MEE INDUSTRIES

Thomas Mee	Co-owner and CEO
D'Arcy Sloane	President and CFO
Dave Sola	Regional Sales Director

PROJECT CONSULTANTS

John Borruso	catalog designer
Vicente Jimenez	Jimenez Construction
Leigh Markopoulos	catalog contributor and managing editor
Henry Urbach	catalog contributor and consulting curator

EXPLORATORIUM PROJECT CONTRIBUTORS

Dennis Bartels, Ph.D.	Executive Director
Bronwyn Bevan, Ph.D.	Associate Director of Program
George Cogan	Chairman, Board of Trustees
Joycelin Craig	Assistant Director, Exhibit Environment
Linda Dackman	Public Information Director
Ann Dabovich	Director for Institutional Advancement
Dana Earl	Assistant Director of Institutional Support
Kari Fox	Development Assistant, Institutional Support
Anne Jennings	Program Relocation Manager
Jeff Hamilton	Director of Community and Government Relations
Van Kasper	Chairman Emeritus, Board of Trustees
Gayle Laird	Photographer
Leslie Patterson	Public Information Officer
Jenny Slafkosky	Public Information Specialist
Silva Raker	Director of Business Development
Phoebe Tookes	Senior Videographer
Kristina Woolsey	Project Director Piers 15/17